Cruise through French vocab with CGP!

If you're aiming for a *bon voyage* through GCSE French,
this nifty CGP Vocab Book is just the ticket.

It covers all the key words you'll need for every topic, with handy
tick boxes to help you keep track of which ones you've learned.

It may be small, but it's perfect for making sure your
GCSE French journey doesn't end in Rouen...

CGP — still the best! ☺

Our sole aim here at CGP is to produce the highest quality books —
carefully written, immaculately presented and dangerously close to being funny.

Then we work our socks off to get them out to you
— at the cheapest possible prices.

Contents

Contents

Published by CGP

Editors:
Rose Jones
Louise McEvoy
Hannah Roscoe
Matt Topping

With thanks to Claire Boulter and Cathy Lear for the proofreading.
With thanks to Jan Greenway for the copyright research.

ISBN: 978 1 78294 861 2

Printed by Elanders Ltd, Newcastle upon Tyne.

Clipart from Corel®

Based on the classic CGP style created by Richard Parsons.

Text, design, layout and original illustrations © Coordination Group Publications Ltd. (CGP) 2018

Colours

blanc	*white*	noir	*black*
bleu	*blue*	noisette	*hazel*
blond	*blond*	pourpre	*purple*
brun	*brown*	rose	*pink*
clair	*light*	rouge	*red*
foncé	*dark*	roux	*red (hair)*
gris	*grey*	vert	*green*
jaune	*yellow*	violet	*purple*
marron	*chestnut, brown*		

Higher only:

vif	*bright*

Common and Useful Words

à l'extérieur	*outside*	complètement	*completely*
à moi	*my, mine*	compter	*to count*
autre	*other*	continuer	*to continue*
ça *Also* cela	*that*	d'ailleurs	*besides*
		de la part de	*on behalf of*
celui-ci	*this one*	doucement	*softly, quietly, slowly*
celui-là	*that one*		
chacun	*each (one)*	s'échapper	*to escape*
changer	*to change*	l'entrée libre *(f)*	*free entry*
chaque	*each*	fermer	*to close*
la chose *Also* le truc	*thing*	informer	*to inform*
		la manière	*manner, way*
complet	*full (no more room)*	le mot	*word*

noter	*to note*	rendre	*to give back, to make (+ adjective)*
occupé	*occupied*		
ouvert	*open*	se rendre compte	*to realise*
ouvrir	*to open*	signifier	*to mean*
par hasard	*by chance*	surtout	*especially, above all*
particulier	*particular, individual*		
quelque chose	*something*	tenir	*to hold*
quelqu'un	*someone*	très	*very*

Higher only:

les connaissances *(f)*   *knowledge*

Comparing Things

beaucoup	*a lot*	mauvais	*bad*
bien	*well*	même	*same*
bon	*good*	moins	*less*
le moins	*the least*	moins que	*less than*
le plus	*the most*	plus	*more*
mal	*badly*	plus que	*more than*

Higher only:

autant	*as much*	le plus mal	*the worst (adverb)*
le meilleur	*the best (adjective)*	meilleur	*better (adjective)*
le mieux	*the best (adverb)*	mieux	*better (adverb)*
le pire	*the worst (adjective)*	pire	*worse (adjective)*
		plus mal	*worse (adverb)*

Conjunctions

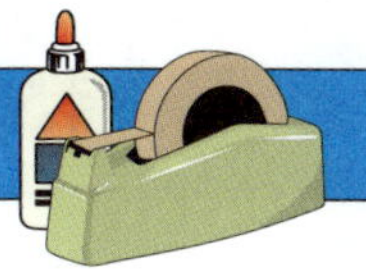

à cause de	*because of*	évidemment	*evidently, obviously*
à part	*apart (from)*	mais	*but*
afin que	*so that*	même si	*even if*
ainsi	*thus, in this way*	ou	*or*
alors	*then, so*	par contre	*on the other hand*
au moins	*at least*	par exemple	*for example*
aussi	*also*	parce que	*because*
car	*because, as*	pendant que	*while*
cependant	*however*	pourtant	*however*
c'est-à-dire	*that's to say*	puis	*then*
comme	*as, like*	puisque	*since*
de l'autre côté	*on the other hand*	sans doute	*without doubt*
donc	*so, therefore*	sauf	*except*
d'un côté	*on the one hand*	si	*if*
ensuite	*then*	y compris	*including*
et	*and*		

Higher only:

dès que   *as soon as*

Days, Months and Seasons

lundi	*Monday*	juin	*June*
mardi	*Tuesday*	juillet	*July*
mercredi	*Wednesday*	août	*August*
jeudi	*Thursday*	septembre	*September*
vendredi	*Friday*	octobre	*October*
samedi	*Saturday*	novembre	*November*
dimanche	*Sunday*	décembre	*December*
janvier	*January*	le printemps	*spring*
février	*February*	l'été *(m)*	*summer*
mars	*March*	l'automne *(m)*	*autumn*
avril	*April*	l'hiver *(m)*	*winter*
mai	*May*		

Greetings and Exclamations

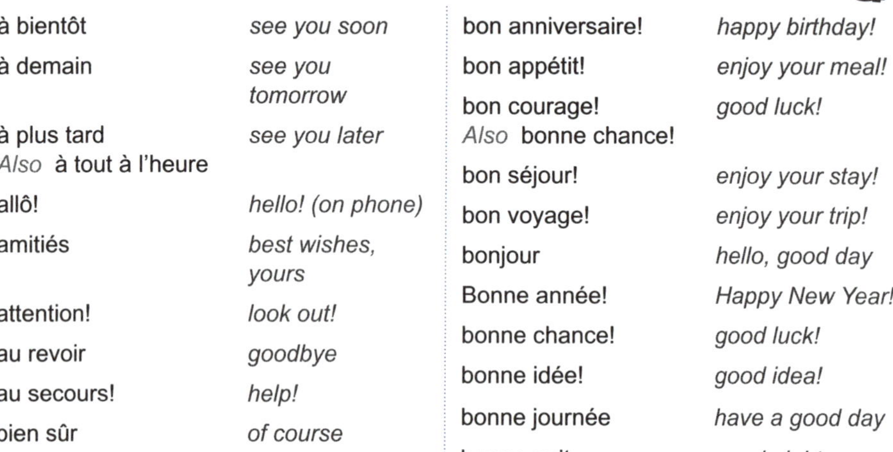

à bientôt	*see you soon*	bon anniversaire!	*happy birthday!*
à demain	*see you tomorrow*	bon appétit!	*enjoy your meal!*
à plus tard Also à tout à l'heure	*see you later*	bon courage! Also bonne chance!	*good luck!*
allô!	*hello! (on phone)*	bon séjour!	*enjoy your stay!*
amitiés	*best wishes, yours*	bon voyage!	*enjoy your trip!*
		bonjour	*hello, good day*
attention!	*look out!*	Bonne année!	*Happy New Year!*
au revoir	*goodbye*	bonne chance!	*good luck!*
au secours!	*help!*	bonne idée!	*good idea!*
bien sûr	*of course*	bonne journée	*have a good day*
bienvenue!	*welcome!*	bonne nuit	*good night*

bonne soirée	*have a good evening*	Mesdames	*ladies*
bonnes vacances!	*have a good holiday!*	Messieurs	*gentlemen*
bonsoir	*good evening*	non	*no*
bravo!	*well done!*	oui	*yes*
ça va	*I'm fine*	pardon	*sorry, pardon*
comme ci comme ça	*so-so*	quel dommage!	*what a shame!*
d'accord	*okay*	salut!	*hi!*
de rien	*you're welcome, it's nothing*	santé!	*cheers!*
désolé	*sorry*	si!	*yes! (after negative)*
excusez-moi	*I'm sorry, excuse me*	s'il te plaît	*please (informal)*
félicitations!	*congratulations!*	s'il vous plaît	*please (formal)*
je t'en prie	*it's a pleasure*	tant mieux!	*all the better!*
Also je vous en prie		tant pis!	*too bad! never mind!*
joyeux Noël	*Merry Christmas*	voici	*here you are*
meilleurs voeux	*best wishes*	voilà	*there you are*
merci	*thank you*	zut!	*damn!*

Higher only:

se serrer la main	*to shake hands*	☹ ☐ ☺ ☐ ☺ ☐

Materials

l'argent (m)	silver	le métal	metal
le béton	concrete	l'or (m)	gold
le bois	wood	le papier	paper
le carton	cardboard	la pierre	stone
le coton	cotton	le plastique	plastic
le cuir	leather	le plomb	lead
le fer	iron	la soie	silk
la laine	wool	le verre	glass

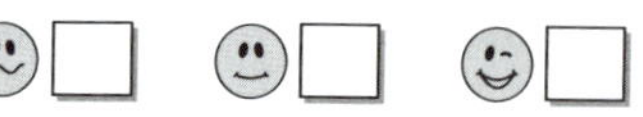

Negatives

moi non plus	me neither	ne…que	only
ne…jamais	never	ne…rien	nothing
ne…personne	no-one, nobody	ni…ni	neither…nor
ne…plus	no longer	pas encore	not yet
ne…pas	not	pas grand-chose	not much

Numbers

un	*one*	le mille	*thousand*
deux	*two*	le million	*million*
trois	*three*	premier	*first*
quatre	*four*	deuxième	*second*
cinq	*five*	troisième	*third*
six	*six*	quatrième	*fourth*
sept	*seven*	cinquième	*fifth*
huit	*eight*	sixième	*sixth*
neuf	*nine*	septième	*seventh*
dix	*ten*	huitième	*eighth*
onze	*eleven*	neuvième	*ninth*
douze	*twelve*	dixième	*tenth*
treize	*thirteen*	la centaine	*about a hundred*
quatorze	*fourteen*	le chiffre	*number (graphical figure)*
quinze	*fifteen*		
seize	*sixteen*	la dizaine	*about ten*
dix-sept	*seventeen*	la douzaine	*dozen*
dix-huit	*eighteen*	le nombre	*number (amount)*
dix-neuf	*nineteen*	nombre de	*several, a good number of*
vingt	*twenty*	nombreux	*numerous*
trente	*thirty*	le numéro	*number (e.g. phone number)*
quarante	*forty*		
cinquante	*fifty*	pas mal de	*quite a few*
soixante	*sixty*	plusieurs	*several*
soixante-dix	*seventy*	tous les deux	*both*
quatre-vingts	*eighty*	tout	*all*
quatre-vingt-dix	*ninety*	la vingtaine	*about twenty*
cent	*hundred*		

Higher only:

ajouter	*to add*

Opinions

à mon avis	*in my opinion*	désagréable	*unpleasant*
absolument	*absolutely*	désirer	*to want, to desire*
affreux	*awful*	détester	*to hate*
agréable	*nice*	la différence	*difference*
aimer	*to like, to love*	différent	*different*
amusant	*fun, amusing*	difficile	*difficult*
avec plaisir	*with pleasure*	dire	*to say*
avoir de la chance	*to be lucky*	d'une grande valeur	*valuable*
bien entendu	*of course, as a matter of course*	efficace	*effective, efficient*
ça dépend	*it depends*	embêtant	*annoying, frustrating*
ça me fait rire	*that makes me laugh*	en avoir marre	*to have had enough*
ça me plaît	*I like that*	en général	*in general*
ça m'énerve	*it gets on my nerves*	enchanté	*delighted (to meet you)*
ça m'est égal	*I don't mind*	ennuyeux *Also* barbant	*boring*
ça ne fait rien	*it doesn't matter*		
ça ne me dit rien	*I don't fancy that, I don't want to*	épouvantable	*dreadful, appalling*
ça suffit	*that's enough*	espérer	*to hope*
casse-pieds	*annoying, a pain in the neck*	étonné	*surprised, astonished*
ce n'est pas la peine	*it's not worth it*	excellent	*excellent*
certain	*certain, sure*	extraordinaire	*extraordinary*
cher	*dear, expensive*	facile	*easy*
chouette	*great*	faible	*weak*
comme ci comme ça	*so-so*	fanatique de	*fanatical about*
compliqué	*complicated*	fantastique	*fantastic*
content	*pleased*	formidable	*great, marvellous*
croire	*to believe, to think*	franchement	*honestly*
		généralement	*generally*

génial	*brilliant*	personnellement	*personally*
grave	*serious*	pessimiste	*pessimistic*
habile	*clever, skilful*	peut-être	*perhaps*
heureusement	*fortunately*	plutôt	*rather*
idéal	*ideal*	populaire	*popular*
incroyable	*unbelievable*	positif	*positive*
inquiet	*worried*	pratique	*practical*
intéressant	*interesting*	préféré *Also* favori	*favourite*
s'intéresser à	*to be interested in*	préférer	*to prefer*
inutile	*useless*	promettre	*to promise*
j'en ai assez *Also* j'en ai marre	*I've had enough*	regretter	*to regret, to be sorry*
joyeux	*merry, joyous*	ridicule	*ridiculous*
magnifique	*magnificent*	satisfait	*satisfied*
malheureusement	*unfortunately*	sembler	*to seem*
marrant	*funny*	sensass	*sensational*
merveilleux	*amazing, marvellous*	simple	*simple*
		stupide	*stupid*
mignon	*cute, sweet*	super	*great*
moche	*ugly, ghastly*	superbe	*superb*
moderne	*modern*	supporter	*to bear, to cope with*
nouveau	*new*		
nul	*no good*	surpris	*surprised*
optimiste	*optimistic*	trouver	*to find*
passionnant	*exciting*	utile	*useful*
la peine	*grief, trouble, effort*	volontiers	*with pleasure*
		vouloir	*to want*
penser	*to think*	vraiment	*really*

Higher only:

l'avis *(m)*	*opinion*	la perte de temps	*waste of time*
être d'accord	*to agree*		

Section 1 — General

Parts of the Body

la bouche	*mouth*	la main	*hand*
le bras	*arm*	le nez	*nose*
le cerveau	*brain*	l'ongle *(f)*	*nail*
les cheveux *(m)*	*hair*	l'oreille *(f)*	*ear*
le coeur	*heart*	l'os *(m)*	*bone*
le corps	*body*	la peau	*skin*
le cou	*neck*	le pied	*foot*
la dent	*tooth*	le sang	*blood*
le doigt	*finger*	la tête	*head*
le dos	*back*	le ventre	*tummy*
l'estomac *(m)*	*stomach*	le visage	*face*
la jambe	*leg*	*Also* la figure	
les lèvres *(f)*	*lips*	la voix	*voice*

Higher only:

le coude	*elbow*	l'oeil *(m)*	*eye*
l'épaule *(f)*	*shoulder*	l'orteil *(m)*	*toe*
le genou	*knee*	*Also* le doigt de pied	
la gorge	*throat*	le poumon	*lung*

Prepositions

à	*at, to*	derrière	*behind*
à côté de	*next to*	devant	*in front (of)*
à partir de	*from (a date or time)*	en	*in, by*
		en dehors de	*outside*
à travers	*across*	en face de	*opposite*
au bord de	*alongside*	entre	*between*
au bout de	*at the end of*	loin de	*far from*
au fond de	*at the bottom of*	malgré	*despite, in spite of*
au lieu de	*instead of*		
au milieu de	*in the middle of*	parmi	*among*
au premier plan	*in the foreground*	pour	*for, in order to*
au-dessous de	*underneath*	près de	*near (to)*
au-dessus de	*above*	sans	*without*
autour de	*around*	selon	*according to*
avec	*with*	*Also* d'après	
contre	*against*	sous	*under*
dans	*in(side)*	sur	*on*
de	*of, from*	vers	*towards, approximately*
depuis	*since*		

Questions

à quelle heure?	*at what time?*	qu'est-ce que?	*what?*
ça s'écrit comment?	*how is it written?*	qu'est-ce que c'est?	*what is it?*
c'est quel jour?	*what day is it?*	qu'est-ce que cela veut dire?	*what does that mean?*
c'est quelle date?	*what is the date?*	qu'est-ce qui?	*what?*
combien?	*how much? how many?*	quand?	*when?*
comment?	*how?*	que?	*what?*
d'où?	*from where?*	que veut dire...?	*what does... mean?*
de quelle couleur	*what colour?*	quel?	*what? which?*
lequel	*which one?*	quelle heure est-il?	*what time is it?*
Also lesquels	*which ones?*	qui?	*who?*
où?	*where?*	quoi?	*what?*
pour combien de temps?	*for how long?*		
pourquoi?	*why?*		

Right and Wrong

avoir raison	*to be right*	nécessaire	*necessary*
avoir tort	*to be wrong*	obligatoire	*obligatory*
corriger	*to correct*	parfait	*perfect*
en fait	*in fact*	sûr	*sure*
l'erreur *(f)*	*error, mistake*	se tromper	*to be wrong, to make a mistake*
la faute	*fault, mistake*		
faux	*false, wrong*	vrai	*true*
juste	*right, fair*		

Shapes, Weights and Measures 

assez	*enough, quite*	le litre	*litre*
bas	*low*	mesurer	*to measure*
beaucoup de	*much, many, a lot of*	le mètre	*metre*
		mince	*thin*
la boîte	*tin, box, can*	la moitié	*half*
la bouteille	*bottle*	le morceau	*piece*
carré	*square*	moyen	*average, middle, medium*
le centilitre	*centilitre*		
le centimètre	*centimetre*	le paquet	*packet*
le cercle	*circle*	peser	*to weigh*
court	*short*	petit	*small, short*
la douzaine	*dozen*	peu	*little*
dur	*hard*	plein	*full*
encore	*more*	la pointure	*shoe size*
étroit	*narrow*	le pot	*jar*
la forme	*shape*	quelques	*some*
le gramme	*gram*	rond	*round*
haut	*high*	suffisamment	*enough, sufficiently*
le hauteur	*height*		
le kilo	*kilo, kilogram*	la taille	*size*
le kilomètre	*kilometre*	le tiers	*third (fraction)*
large	*wide*	la tranche	*slice*
léger	*light*	trop	*too*

Higher only:

à peine	*hardly*	lourd	*heavy*

Time Expressions

à la fois	*at once*	d'habitude	*usually*
à l'avenir	*in the future*	durer	*to last*
à l'heure	*on time*	en attendant	*in the meantime*
à temps partiel	*part time*	en avance	*in advance*
actuel	*present, current*	en ce moment	*at the moment*
actuellement	*at the present time, currently*	en même temps	*at the same time*
		en retard	*late (for something)*
l'an *(m)* Also l'année *(f)*	*year*	en train de	*in the process of*
après	*after*	encore une fois	*once again*
après-demain	*the day after tomorrow*	enfin	*finally, at last*
		environ	*about*
l'après-midi *(m)*	*afternoon*	être en train de	*to be in the process of*
au début	*at the start*		
aujourd'hui	*today*	être sur le point de	*to be about to*
auparavant	*beforehand*	la fin	*end*
autrefois	*formerly*	finalement	*finally*
avant	*before*	la fois	*time (occurrence)*
avant-hier	*the day before yesterday*	hebdomadaire	*weekly*
		l'heure *(f)*	*hour, time*
bientôt	*soon*	hier	*yesterday*
d'abord	*first of all*	il y a	*ago*
la date	*date*	l'instant *(m)*	*moment, instant*
de bonne heure	*on time, early*	le jour Also la journée	*day*
de nouveau	*again, once more*		
de temps en temps	*from time to time*	jusqu'à	*until*
le début	*start, beginning*	le lendemain	*the next day*
déjà	*already*	longtemps	*(for) a long time*
demain	*tomorrow*	maintenant	*now*
demi	*half*	le matin	*morning*
dernier	*last*	la matinée	*morning*
deux fois	*twice*	mensuel	*monthly*

midi	*noon, lunchtime*	la saison	*season*
minuit	*midnight*	la seconde	*second*
la minute	*minute*	la semaine	*week*
le mois	*month*	seulement	*only*
normalement	*normally*	le siècle	*century*
la nuit	*night*	le soir *Also* la soirée	*evening*
passé	*last, just gone*		
le passé	*past*	soudain	*sudden(ly)*
pendant	*during*	souvent	*often*
plus tard	*later*	suivant	*following*
pour l'instant	*for the moment*	sur le point de	*on the point of*
presque	*almost*	tard	*late*
prochain	*next*	tôt	*early*
le quart	*quarter*	toujours	*always, still*
quelquefois *Also* parfois	*sometimes*	tous les jours	*every day*
		tout à coup *Also* tout d'un coup	*all of a sudden, suddenly*
la quinzaine *Also* les quinze jours *(m)*	*fortnight*	tout de suite	*straight away*
		une fois	*once*
rarement	*rarely*	la veille	*day before, eve*
récemment	*recently*	vite	*quickly*
récent	*recent*	le week-end	*weekend*
le retard	*delay*		

Higher only:

instantané	*instantaneous*	venir de	*to have just*

Abbreviations

la BD (bande-dessinée)	*comic book*
le CDI (centre de documentation et d'information)	*school library*
le CES (collège d'enseignement secondaire)	*secondary school*
les DOM *(m)* (départements d'outre-mer)	*French departments overseas*
l'EMT *(f)* (éducation manuelle et technique)	*D&T, CDT*
l'EPS *(f)* (éducation physique et sportive)	*PE*
l'HLM *(f)* (habitation à loyer modéré)	*council flat, council house*
la MJC (maison des jeunes et de la culture)	*youth club and arts centre*
P et T	*post office and tele-communications service*
le RER (réseau express régional)	*commuter train service*
la RN (route nationale)	*main road*
le SAMU (service d'aide médicale d'urgence)	*ambulance service*
le SDF (sans domicile fixe)	*homeless person*
la SNCF (société nationale des chemins de fer français)	*French national railway company*
SVP (s'il vous plaît)	*please*
le TGV (train à grande vitesse)	*high speed train*
la TVA (taxe sur valeur ajoutée)	*VAT*
l'UE *(f)* (Union Européenne)	*EU*
le VTT (vélo tout terrain)	*mountain bike, mountain biking*

Animals

l'animal *(m)*	*animal*		la mouche	*fly*
l'animal domestique *(m)*	*pet*		le mouton	*sheep*
le chat	*cat*		l'oiseau *(m)*	*bird*
le cheval	*horse*		le poisson rouge	*goldfish*
le chien	*dog*		le poisson tropical	*tropical fish*
le cochon	*pig*		le serpent	*snake*
le cochon d'Inde	*guinea pig*		la souris	*mouse*
le hamster	*hamster*		la tortue	*tortoise*
le lapin	*rabbit*		la vache	*cow*

Clothes

à la mode	*fashionable*		la chaussette	*sock*
à pois	*spotty*		la chaussure	*shoe*
l'anneau *(m)*	*ring*		la chemise	*shirt*
Also la bague			la chemise de nuit	*nightie*
les bijoux *(m)*	*jewellery*		le collant	*tights*
le blouson	*jacket (casual)*		le collier	*necklace*
la botte	*boot*		le complet	*three-piece suit*
les boucles d'oreille *(f)*	*earrings*		la couleur	*colour*
le bracelet	*bracelet*		la cravate	*tie*
le caleçon	*boxers*		la culotte	*knickers*
la casquette	*cap*		démodé	*old-fashioned*
la ceinture	*belt*		de taille moyenne	*medium*
le chapeau	*hat*		l'écharpe *(f)*	*scarf*

enlever *Also* ôter	*to take off,* *to remove*	le piercing à l'oreille	*ear piercing*
les fringues *(f)*	*clothes*	la poche	*pocket*
le gant	*glove*	le polo	*polo shirt*
le gilet	*cardigan*	le pull	*sweater, jumper*
il te va bien	*it suits you*	le pyjama	*pyjamas*
l'imper(méable) *(m)*	*waterproof*	rayé	*stripy*
le jean	*jeans*	rétro	*retro*
la jupe	*skirt*	la robe	*dress*
le lin	*linen*	le rouge à lèvres	*lipstick*
les lunettes de soleil *(f)*	*sunglasses*	le sac	*bag*
le maillot de bain	*swimsuit, trunks*	le sac à main	*handbag*
le maillot de sport	*sports shirt*	le short	*shorts*
le manteau	*coat*	le slip	*underpants*
le maquillage	*make-up*	le soutien-gorge	*bra*
la mode	*fashion*	le style	*style*
la montre	*watch*	le survêtement	*tracksuit*
le mouchoir	*tissue,* *handkerchief*	la tenue de sport	*sports kit*
		le tricot	*jumper*
la paire	*pair*	le t-shirt	*T-shirt*
le pantalon	*trousers*	la veste	*jacket*
le parapluie	*umbrella*	les vêtements *(m)*	*clothes*
		vêtu de	*dressed in*

Higher only:

le casque	*helmet*	se faire couper les cheveux	*to have your hair cut*
le chapeau de paille	*straw hat*		
le chemisier	*blouse*	le foulard	*scarf*
le costume	*suit*	le képi	*military cap*
la couture	*sewing, tailoring*	se maquiller	*to put on make-up*
emprunter	*to borrow*		
se faire coiffer	*to have your hair done*	les pantoufles *(f)*	*slippers*
		le pull à capuche	*hoody,* *hooded top*

Section 2 — Identity & Culture

la robe de chambre	*dressing gown*	le trou	*hole*
serré	*tight*	le velours	*velvet*
teint	*dyed*		

Daily Routine

apporter	*to bring*	habituel	*usual*
la brosse à dents	*toothbrush*	laver	*to wash*
se brosser les dents	*to brush your teeth*	se laver	*to have a wash*
commencer	*to begin*	se lever	*to get up, to stand up*
se coucher	*to go to bed*	organiser	*to organise*
le dentifrice	*toothpaste*	se raser	*to shave*
se déshabiller	*to get undressed, to undress*	le réveil	*alarm clock*
dormir	*to sleep*	se réveiller	*to wake up*
se doucher	*to have a shower*	le sèche-cheveux	*hair dryer*
faire la cuisine	*to do the cooking*	la serviette	*towel*
finir	*to finish, to end*	la vie	*life*
s'habiller	*to get dressed*		

Higher only:

avoir sommeil	*to be sleepy*	quotidien	*daily*
faire la grasse matinée	*to have a lie in*		

Describing People

avoir	*to have*	laid	*ugly*
la barbe	*beard*	long	*long*
barbu	*bearded*	les lunettes *(f)*	*glasses*
beau	*beautiful*	maigre	*thin*
bouclé	*wavy, curly*	le mec	*guy*
la célébrité *Also* la star	*celebrity*	mi-long	*medium length*
châtain	*brown (hair)*	la moustache	*moustache*
chauve	*bald*	musulman	*Muslim*
chrétien	*Christian*	normal	*normal*
de bonne humeur	*in a good mood*	pareil	*the same*
de mauvaise humeur	*in a bad mood*	se plaindre	*to complain*
décrire	*to describe*	plus âgé	*older*
en bonne forme	*fit*	le poids	*weight*
enceinte	*pregnant*	raide	*straight (hair)*
être	*to be*	reconnu	*well-known*
le fils unique *Also* la fille unique	*only child*	la religion	*religion*
frisé	*frizzy, curly*	sensationnel *Also* sensass	*sensational*
grand	*tall*	le sens de l'humour	*sense of humour*
gros	*fat*	la sorte	*type*
l'humeur *(f)*	*mood*	sourd	*deaf*
joli	*pretty*	le tatouage	*tattoo*
juif	*Jewish*	triste	*sad*
		les yeux *(m)*	*eyes*

Higher only:

élégant	*elegant*	la foi	*faith*
l'esprit *(m)*	*wit, intelligence*	le genre	*type*
étonnant	*surprising*	habillé	*dressed*
étrange	*strange*	maladroit	*clumsy*

se mettre en colère	*to get angry*	retraité	*retired*
le modèle	*role model*	le sexe	*gender*
ondulé	*wavy*	similaire	*similar*
ressembler à	*to look like, to resemble*		

Eating Out

à la carte	*from the menu, à la carte*	le goût	*taste*
l'addition *(f)*	*bill*	grillé	*grilled*
l'alcool *(m)*	*alcohol*	le hors-d'oeuvre	*starter*
l'assiette *(f)*	*plate*	le menu à prix fixe	*fixed price menu*
l'auberge *(f)*	*inn*	le parfum	*flavour*
la bière	*beer*	partager	*to share*
la boisson	*drink*	payer	*to pay*
la carte	*menu*	la petite cuillère	*teaspoon*
le casse-croûte	*snack*	la pizzeria	*pizzeria*
commander	*to order*	le plat	*dish*
compris	*included*	le plat du jour	*dish of the day*
la côtelette	*chop*	le plat principal	*main course*
le couteau	*knife*	le poivre	*pepper*
les couverts *(m)*	*cutlery*	le pourboire	*tip*
la cuillère Also la cuiller	*spoon*	le repas	*meal*
		le restaurant	*restaurant*
cuit	*cooked*	le salon de thé	*tea room*
le dessert	*dessert*	le sel	*salt*
l'entrecôte *(f)*	*steak*	le self-service	*self-service*
la fourchette	*fork*	service compris	*service included*
le glacier	*ice cream parlour*	service non compris	*service not included*

servir	*to serve*	le verre	*glass*
la spécialité	*speciality*	le vin	*wine*
le supplément	*supplement*		

Higher only:

à point	*medium (meat)*	épais	*thick*
l'apéritif *(m)*	*aperitif, drink before a meal*	l'huître *(f)*	*oyster*
appétissant	*appetising*	piquant *Also* épicé	*hot, spicy*
bien cuit	*well done (meat)*	le plateau	*tray*
la brasserie	*bar-restaurant*	saignant	*rare (meat)*

Family

s'appeler	*to be called*	le cousin *Also* la cousine	*cousin*
le beau-fils	*son-in-law*		
le beau-frère	*stepbrother, brother-in-law*	le demi-frère	*half-brother*
		la demi-sœur	*half-sister*
le beau-père	*stepfather, father-in-law*	l'enfant *(m/f)*	*child*
le bébé	*baby*	la famille	*family*
		la fille	*daughter*
la belle-fille	*daughter-in-law*	le fils	*son*
la belle-mère	*stepmother, mother-in-law*	le frère	*brother*
		les frères jumeaux *(m)*	*twin brothers*
la belle-sœur	*stepsister, sister-in-law*	la grand-mère	*grandmother*
cadet	*younger (brother, sister)*	le grand-père	*grandfather*

les grands-parents *(m)*	*grandparents*	le papa	*dad*
le jumeau	*twin (male)*	le papy *Also* le pépé	*granddad*
la jumelle	*twin (female)*		
la maman	*mum*	les parents *(m)*	*parents*
la mamie *Also* la mémé	*grandma*	le père	*father*
		le petit-enfant	*grandchild*
marié	*married*	le petit-fils	*grandson*
se marier	*to get married*	la petite-fille	*granddaughter*
le membre de la famille	*family member*	la responsabilité	*responsibility*
la mère	*mother*	la sœur	*sister*
né le...	*born on the*	les sœurs jumelles *(f)*	*twin sisters*
le neveu	*nephew*	se souvenir de	*to remember*
la nièce	*niece*	la tante	*aunt*
l'oncle *(m)*	*uncle*	unique	*only (child)*
		le voisin	*neighbour*

Higher only:

adopté	*adopted*	la mère célibataire	*single mother*
le baptême	*christening*	le parent	*relation*
le fiancé *Also* la fiancée	*fiancé(e)*	le père célibataire	*single father*
		surveiller	*to watch, to keep an eye on*
gâter	*to spoil (a child)*	les vrais jumeaux *(m)*	*identical twins*

Fruit and Veg 

l'abricot *(m)*	apricot	le melon	melon
l'ananas *(m)*	pineapple	l'oignon *(m)*	onion
la banane	banana	l'orange *(f)*	orange
la carotte	carrot	le pamplemousse	grapefruit
la cerise	cherry	la pêche	peach
le champignon	mushroom	les petits-pois *(m)*	peas
le chou	cabbage	la poire	pear
le chou de Bruxelles	Brussels sprout	le poivron	pepper
le chou-fleur	cauliflower	la pomme	apple
le citron	lemon	la pomme de terre	potato
les crudités *(f)*	raw vegetables	pourri	rotten
la fraise	strawberry	la prune	plum
la framboise	raspberry	le radis	radish
le fruit	fruit	le raisin	grape
le haricot	bean	la salade	lettuce, salad
le haricot vert	green bean	la tomate	tomato
le légume	vegetable		

Higher only:

l'ail *(m)*	garlic	la laitue	lettuce
l'artichaut *(m)*	artichoke	mûr	ripe
le concombre	cucumber	le poireau	leek
les épinards	spinach		

Going Out

à l'appareil	*on the line, speaking*	immédiatement	*immediately*
appeler	*to call*	l'invitation *(f)*	*invitation*
arriver	*to arrive*	inviter	*to invite*
le bar	*bar*	raconter	*to tell*
la boîte de nuit	*nightclub*	remettre	*to put back, to postpone*
le coup de téléphone	*telephone call*	rencontrer	*to meet*
se dépêcher	*to hurry*	rendre visite à	*to visit (a person)*
la discothèque	*disco*	sonner	*to ring*
entendre	*to hear*	téléphoner	*to phone*
le faux numéro	*wrong number*		

Higher only:

annuler	*to cancel*	l'événement *(m)*	*event*
le bip sonore	*tone*	le feu d'artifice	*fireworks*
le combiné	*receiver*	l'indicatif *(m)*	*area code*
composer le numéro	*to dial the number*	la messagerie vocale	*voice mail*

Leisure

French	English
accompagner	*to accompany, to go with*
l'activité *(f)*	*activity*
aller	*to go*
l'alpinisme *(m)*	*mountaineering*
s'amuser	*to enjoy oneself*
l'appel *(m)*	*call*
avoir lieu	*to take place*
la bande dessinée	*comic*
la bicyclette	*bicycle*
le billet	*ticket*
bon marché	*cheap*
les boules *(f)*	*boules*
le bowling	*bowling*
le bureau des objets trouvés	*lost property office*
le centre de loisirs	*leisure centre*
choisir	*to choose*
le cinéma	*cinema*
le club	*club*
le club des jeunes	*youth club*
la collection	*collection*
collectionner	*to collect*
la console de jeux	*games console*
la danse	*dancing*
danser	*to dance*
débuter	*to begin*
dessiner	*to draw*
les distractions *(f)*	*things to do*
le divertissement	*entertainment*
donner	*to give*
les échecs *(m)*	*chess*
ensemble	*together*
envoyer	*to send*
l'escalade *(f)*	*climbing*
faire	*to do*
faire de l'équitation Also faire du cheval	*to go horse riding*
faire de l'exercice	*to exercise*
faire de la voile	*to sail*
faire des randonnées	*to hike*
faire du bowling	*to go bowling*
faire du patin à roulettes	*to roller-skate*
faire du skate	*to skateboard*
faire partie de	*to be a member of*
fêter	*to celebrate*
l'histoire d'espionnage *(f)*	*spy story*
l'inconvénient *(m)* Also le désavantage	*disadvantage*
s'intéresser à	*to be interested in*
le jeu	*game*
le jeu de cartes	*card game*
le jeu de société	*board game*
le jeu électronique	*electronic game*
le jeu vidéo	*video game*
le jouet	*toy*
le lecteur DVD	*DVD player*
le lecteur MP3	*MP3 player*
libre	*free (unoccupied)*
lire	*to read*
le loisir	*leisure*

les loisirs	*free-time activities*	se reposer	*to rest*
le magazine *Also* la revue	*magazine*	retourner	*to go back (somewhere for a second time)*
le membre	*member*	le risque	*risk*
participer à	*to take part in*	le roman policier	*crime novel*
le passe-temps	*pastime, hobby*	la salle de jeux	*games room*
passer du temps	*to spend time*	la séance	*sitting, viewing (e.g. cinema)*
la pêche	*fishing*	sortir	*to go out*
peindre	*to paint*	le spectateur	*spectator*
le pique-nique	*picnic*	la surprise-partie	*surprise party*
le plaisir	*pleasure*	le temps libre	*free time*
le portable	*mobile (phone)*	le terrain de jeux	*play area*
promener	*to take for a walk (e.g. dog)*	le texto	*text message*
se promener	*to go for a walk*	le théâtre	*theatre*
regarder	*to watch, to look at*	le vélo	*bike*
remplir	*to fill*	venir	*to come*
se rencontrer	*to meet*	voir	*to see*
rentrer	*to go back (e.g. home)*		

Higher only:

s'abonner	*to subscribe*	féliciter	*to congratulate*
l'ennui *(m)*	*boredom*	la tournée	*tour, round*
expérimenter	*to experience*	le voilier	*sailing boat*

Media

les actualités *(f)*	*news*	le film de fantaisie	*fantasy film*
l'affiche *(f)*	*poster, notice*	le film de guerre	*war film*
l'annonce *(f)*	*advert, notice*	le film de science-fiction	*science fiction film*
l'avantage *(m)*	*advantage*	le film policier	*detective film*
la chaîne	*channel (TV), station (radio)*	le film romantique	*romantic film, rom com*
classique	*classical*	l'idée *(f)*	*idea*
la comédie	*comedy*	les informations *(f)*	*news, information*
la comédie dramatique	*drama*	le jeu télévisé	*game show*
le dessin animé	*cartoon*	le journal	*newspaper*
le dictionnaire	*dictionary*	le journal télévisé	*TV news*
le documentaire	*documentary*	la lecture	*reading*
doublé	*dubbed*	la pièce de théâtre	*play (at the theatre)*
l'émission *(f)*	*programme*	le polar	*crime film*
l'émission jeunesse *(f)*	*children's programme*	la publicité	*advert*
l'émission musicale *(f)*	*music programme*	réel	*real*
l'émission sportive *(f)*	*sports programme*	le roman	*novel*
l'exposition *(f)*	*exhibition*	la scène	*stage*
le feuilleton	*soap opera*	la série	*series*
le film	*film*	le site	*website*
le film à suspense	*thriller*	la téléréalité	*reality TV*
le film d'action	*action film*	la télévision *Also* la télé	*television*
le film d'aventure	*adventure film*	la télévision par câble	*cable TV*
le film d'épouvante	*horror film*	la vedette	*star, celebrity*
le film d'horreur	*horror film*	le western	*western*

Higher only:

bref	*brief*	il s'agit de	*it's about*
la comédie de situation	*sitcom*	les sous-titres *(m)*	*subtitles*
les effets spéciaux *(m)*	*special effects*	la télécommande	*remote control*
en différé	*pre-recorded*	la télévision satellite	*satellite TV*
en direct	*live*		

Music

la batterie	*drums*	la musique	*music*
la chaîne hi-fi	*stereo system*	la musique classique	*classical music*
la chanson	*song*	la musique folk	*folk music*
chanter	*to sing*	la musique pop	*pop music*
le chanteur	*singer*	la musique rap	*rap music*
Also la chanteuse		la musique rock	*rock music*
la clarinette	*clarinet*	l'orchestre *(m)*	*orchestra*
le concert	*concert*	le piano	*piano*
le disque compact	*CD*	le saxophone	*saxophone*
le festival de musique	*music festival*	le spectacle	*show*
la flûte	*flute*	la trompette	*trumpet*
la flûte à bec	*recorder*	la version originale	*original version*
le groupe	*group*	le violon	*violin*
la guitare	*guitar*		

Higher only:

la comédie musicale	*musical*	la mélodie	*melody*
les écouteurs *(m)*	*earphones, headphones*		

Personal Information

l'adresse *(f)*	*address*	moi-même	*myself*
l'adulte *(m/f)*	*adult*	Monsieur	*Mr*
l'âge *(m)*	*age*	monsieur	*sir*
aîné	*older, first born*	mort	*dead*
l'anniversaire *(m)*	*birthday*	la naissance	*birth*
la carte d'identité	*identity card*	la nationalité	*nationality*
célèbre	*famous*	né	*born*
célibataire	*single*	le nom de jeune fille	*maiden name*
la date de naissance	*date of birth*	le nom	*surname*
divorcé	*divorced*	Also le nom de famille	
le garçon	*boy*	le passeport	*passport*
les gens *(m)*	*people*	pauvre	*poor*
l'homme *(m)*	*man*	la personne	*person*
l'identité *(f)*	*identity*	la pièce d'identité	*proof of ID*
jeune	*young*	porter	*to wear, to carry*
le lieu	*place*	le prénom	*first name*
le lieu de naissance	*place of birth*	religieux	*religious*
loger	*to stay (in a hotel), to live*	riche	*rich*
		sans travail	*unemployed*
Madame	*Mrs*	signer	*to sign*
madame	*madam*	le surnom	*nickname*
Mademoiselle	*Miss*	timide	*shy*
mademoiselle	*miss, young lady*	tranquille	*quiet*
		vieux	*old*

Higher only:

à la retraite	*retired*	naître	*to be born*

Personalities

animé	*lively*		impoli	*impolite, rude*
autoritaire	*bossy*		indépendant	*independent*
aventureux	*adventurous*		insupportable	*unbearable*
avoir l'air	*to seem*		intelligent	*intelligent*
bête	*stupid*		négatif	*negative*
le bonheur	*happiness*		la personnalité	*personality*
le caractère	*character, personality*		poli	*polite*
			raisonnable	*reasonable*
charmant	*charming*		rigolo	*funny*
chic	*smart*		sage	*wise, well behaved*
confiant	*confident*			
craintif	*timid, fearful*		sérieux	*serious*
drôle	*funny*		sévère	*strict*
égoïste	*selfish*		silencieux	*silent, quiet*
généreux	*generous*		strict	*strict*
honnête	*honest*		têtu	*stubborn*
impatient	*impatient*			

Higher only:

à l'aise	*at ease*		gâté	*spoilt*
agaçant	*annoying*		jaloux	*jealous*
compréhensif	*understanding*		nerveux	*nervous*
effronté	*cheeky*		prétentieux	*pretentious*
fiable	*reliable*		sensible	*sensitive*
fidèle	*loyal*		sûr de soi	*self-confident*
fier	*proud*		le trait	*trait*
fou	*mad*		vaniteux	*vain*

Relationships

accepter	*to accept*	éviter	*to avoid*
adorer	*to love*	s'excuser	*to apologise*
agacer	*to annoy*	expliquer	*to explain*
aimable	*likeable*	fâché	*angry*
l'ami *(m)*	*friend (male)*	*Also* en colère	
Also le copain		se fâcher	*to get angry*
amical	*friendly*	faire la connaissance	*to get to know*
l'amie *(f)*	*friend (female)*	la femme	*wife*
Also la copine		*Also* l'épouse *(f)*	
l'amitié *(f)*	*friendship*	gentil	*kind*
l'amour *(m)*	*love*	s'habituer à	*to get used to*
apprécier	*to appreciate*	heureux	*happy*
attendre	*to wait for*	la honte	*shame*
avoir envie de	*to fancy*	introduire	*to introduce*
le baiser	*kiss*	malheureux	*unhappy, unlucky*
battre	*to beat, to hit*	le mari	*husband*
bavard	*talkative*	*Also* l'époux *(m)*	
bavarder	*to chat*	le mariage	*marriage, wedding*
compter sur	*to count on*	méchant	*nasty, fierce*
connaître	*to know (be familiar with)*	les nouvelles *(f)*	*news (what someone's been up to)*
contribuer	*to contribute*		
le correspondant	*pen friend*	oublier	*to forget*
Also la correspondante		pardonner	*to forgive*
critiquer	*to criticise*	le partenaire	*partner*
discuter	*to discuss*	*Also* la partenaire	
se disputer	*to argue*	pénible	*awful, painful*
divorcer	*to divorce*	le petit ami	*boyfriend*
écrire	*to write*	*Also* le copain	
s'entendre avec	*to get on with*	la petite amie	*girlfriend*
s'entendre bien (avec)	*to get on well (with)*	*Also* la copine	

plaire	*to please*	respecter	*to respect*
plaisanter	*to joke*	rester en contact	*to stay in touch*
pleurer	*to cry*	rire	*to laugh*
présenter	*to present*	le sens de l'humour	*sense of humour*
se présenter	*to introduce oneself*	le sentiment	*feeling*
		séparé	*separated*
prêter	*to lend*	se séparer	*to separate*
se rappeler	*to remember*	seul	*alone*
les rapports *(m)*	*relationships*	sourire	*to smile*
refuser	*to refuse, to say no*	sympa	*nice, friendly*
		tchatter	*to chat*
remercier	*to thank*	la vérité	*truth*
le rendez-vous	*meeting, appointment*		

Higher only:

l'alliance *(f)*	*wedding ring*	le fiancé *Also* la fiancée	*fiancé(e)*
cacher	*to hide*		
le conseil	*advice*	gêner	*to embarrass, to bother, to disturb*
coupable	*guilty*		
déçu	*disappointed*	humilier	*to humiliate*
déranger	*to disturb*	mentir	*to lie*
la dispute	*argument*	mépriser	*to despise*
douter	*to doubt*	les noces *(f)*	*wedding*
épouser	*to marry*	reconnaissant	*grateful*
exprès	*on purpose*	tomber amoureux (de)	*to fall in love (with)*
les fiançailles *(f)*	*engagement*		

Shopping

acheter	*to buy*	l'épicerie *(f)*	*grocer's*
l'argent *(m)*	*money*	faire des achats	*to shop*
l'argent de poche *(m)*	*pocket money*	faire des économies	*to save money*
avoir besoin de	*to need*	faire du lèche-vitrines	*to go window-shopping*
la banque	*bank*	faire les courses	*to go shopping (food)*
la bijouterie	*jeweller's*		
la boucherie	*butcher's*	faire les magasins	*to go shopping (in town)*
la boulangerie	*baker's*	*Also* faire du shopping	
la cabine d'essayage	*changing room*	la garantie	*guarantee*
le cadeau	*present*	garantir	*to guarantee*
la caisse	*till*	le grand magasin	*department store*
la carte bancaire	*bank card*	gratuit	*free (no charge)*
la carte de crédit	*credit card*	le kiosque à journaux	*newsstand*
cassé	*broken*	laisser	*to leave (an object)*
le centre commercial	*shopping centre*		
la charcuterie	*cooked meats shop, delicatessen*	la librairie	*book shop*
		la livraison	*delivery*
		la livre sterling	*pound sterling*
le chèque	*cheque*	le magasin	*shop*
le choix	*choice*	*Also* la boutique	
le client	*customer*	le magasin de chaussures	*shoe shop*
le coin	*corner*		
les commerces *(m)*	*shops*	le magasin d'électroménager	*electrical goods shop*
coûter	*to cost*		
dépenser	*to spend*	le magasin de mode	*clothes shop*
disponible	*available*	le marchand	*market trader*
d'occasion	*second hand*	le marché	*market*
la droguerie	*hardware shop*	la marque	*brand, make*
échanger	*to swap, to exchange*	le mode de paiement	*payment method*
		la monnaie	*change*
l'endommagement *(m)*	*damage*	neuf	*brand new*

le panier	*basket*	le rayon	*department*
la parfumerie	*perfume shop*	le reçu	*receipt*
la pâtisserie	*cake shop*	la réduction	*reduction*
la pièce de remplacement	*replacement part*	réduit	*reduced*
		remplacer	*to replace*
la plainte	*complaint*	la réparation	*repair*
le portefeuille	*wallet*	les soldes *(m)*	*sales*
le porte-monnaie	*purse*	le supermarché	*supermarket*
la poste	*post office*	le tabac	*tobacconist, newsagent*
pousser	*to push*		
le prix	*price*	la valeur	*value*
le produit de remplacement	*replacement product*	vendre	*to sell*
		la vente	*sale*
les provisions *(f)*	*food shopping*	la vitrine	*window*

Higher only:

l'assurance *(f)*	*insurance*	le nettoyage à sec	*dry cleaning*
le commerçant	*shop keeper*	la poissonnerie	*fishmonger's*
la grande surface	*superstore*	le pressing	*dry cleaner's*
l'hypermarché *(m)*	*hypermarket*	la quincaillerie	*ironmonger's*
la laverie automatique	*launderette*	ramener	*to take back*
le libre-service	*self-service*	rapporter	*to take back*
le mode d'emploi	*instructions*	rembourser	*to refund*

Sport

l'arbitre *(m)*	*referee*	le football *Also* le foot	*football*
les arts martiaux *(m)*	*martial arts*	frapper	*to knock, to hit*
assister à	*to attend*	gagner	*to win, to earn*
l'athlétisme *(m)*	*athletics*	grimper	*to climb*
le badminton	*badminton*	la gymnastique	*gymnastics*
la balle	*ball (small)*	le handball	*handball*
le ballon	*ball (large)*	le hockey	*hockey*
le basket	*basketball*	les jeux Olympiques *(m)*	*Olympics*
les baskets *(m)*	*trainers*	jouer	*to play*
le boxe	*boxing*	le joueur	*player*
le canoë-kayak	*canoeing, kayaking*	le judo	*judo*
le centre sportif *Also* le centre de sport	*sports centre*	le karaté	*karate*
le championnat	*championship*	marquer un but	*to score a goal*
le concours	*competition*	le match nul	*draw (match result)*
le coup de pied	*kick*	nager	*to swim*
la coupe du monde	*world cup*	la natation	*swimming*
courir	*to run*	le parachutage	*parachuting*
la course	*race*	la parapente	*paragliding*
crier	*to shout*	le patin à glace	*ice skating*
le cyclisme	*cycling*	le patin à roulettes	*roller skate, roller-skating*
le cycliste	*cyclist*	le patinage	*skating*
s'entraîner	*to train*	patiner	*to skate*
l'équipe *(f)*	*team*	la patinoire	*ice rink*
l'équipement *(m)*	*equipment*	la pétanque	*petanque*
l'équitation *(f)*	*horse riding*	la piscine	*swimming pool*
essayer	*to try*	la planche à voile	*windsurfing*
faire de la gymnastique	*to do gymnastics*		
faire du sport	*to do sport*		

recevoir	to receive, to be host to
le roller	roller-blading
le rugby	rugby
sauter	to jump
le skate	skateboarding
le ski	skiing
le ski nautique	waterskiing
le sport	sport
sportif	sporty
les sports d'hiver (m)	winter sports
les sports extrêmes (m)	extreme sports
les sports nautiques (m)	water sports
le squash	squash

le stade	stadium
le surf	surfing
surfer	to surf
le tennis	tennis
le tennis de table	table tennis
le terrain	pitch (sports)
toucher	to touch
le trampoline	trampolining
le vestiaire	changing room
la victoire	win, victory
la voile	sailing
le volley	volleyball

Higher only:

les articles de sport (m)	sports equipment
l'aviron (m)	rowing
la canne à pêche	fishing rod
contrôler	to control, to test
l'entraînement	training
l'escrime (f)	fencing
lancer	to throw, to launch
la ligue	league
le maillot de sport	sports shirt, jersey

marquer un essai	to score a try
la mi-temps	half-time, halt (of a sports match)
la planche de surf	surf board
la plongée sous-marine	deep-sea diving
la rencontre sportive	sports event
le tir à l'arc	archery
le tournoi	tournament

Technology

l'adresse email *(f)*	*email address*
à l'attention de	*for the attention of*
le blog	*blog*
le bon numéro	*correct number*
charger	*to load*
le clavier	*keyboard*
cliquer	*to click*
coller	*to stick, to paste*
contacter	*to contact*
le cyber harcèlement	*cyber bullying*
la disquette	*disc*
l'écran *(m)*	*screen*
l'électricité *(f)*	*electricity*
l'email *(m)* *Also* le courrier électronique *Also* le courriel	*email*
en ligne	*online*
la façon	*way (of doing something)*
fonctionner	*to work (function)*
le forum de discussion	*chatroom*
l'imprimante *(f)*	*printer*
imprimer	*to print*
l'inconvénient *(m)*	*disadvantage*
lent	*slow*
le logiciel	*software*
le message	*message*
mettre en ligne	*to put online*
le mot de passe	*password*
numérique	*digital*
le numéro de téléphone	*phone number*
l'ordinateur *(m)*	*computer*
l'ordinateur portable *(m)*	*laptop*
l'ordinateur tablette *(m)*	*tablet*
la page web *Also* la page internet	*webpage*
le répondeur	*answer phone*
le réseau social	*social network*
le site web *Also* le site internet	*website*
surfer sur internet	*to surf the internet*
taper	*to type*
la technologie	*technology*
télécharger	*to download*
le téléphone	*phone*
la toile *Also* le web	*internet*
la touche	*key (of keyboard)*
le virus	*virus*
la webcam	*webcam*
la Xbox®	*Xbox®*

Higher only:

appuyer	*to press*	l'icône *(f)*	*icon*
la base de données	*database*	l'internaute *(m)*	*internet user*
le blogueur	*blogger*	le lien	*link*
Also la blogueuse		le moniteur	*monitor*
le bouton	*button*	la page d'accueil	*homepage*
la caméra	*video camera*	la pile	*battery*
le caméscope	*camcorder*	le réseau	*network*
la carte mémoire	*memory card*	sauvegarder	*to back up*
le compte	*account*	le slash	*forward slash*
le disque dur	*hard drive*	le tiret bas	*underscore*
l'écran tactile *(m)*	*touch screen*	le traitement de texte	*word processing*
effacer	*to erase, to rub out*	le webmail	*webmail*
enregistrer	*to record, to save*		

Things to Drink

boire	*to drink*	l'eau minérale *(f)*	*mineral water*
le cacao	*cocoa*	l'eau potable *(f)*	*drinking water*
le café	*café, coffee*	le jus	*juice*
la cafetière	*cafetière*	le jus de fruit	*fruit juice*
le champagne	*champagne*	le lait	*milk*
le chocolat chaud	*hot chocolate*	la limonade	*lemonade*
le cidre	*cider*	la soif	*thirst*
le coca	*coke*	la tasse	*cup*
l'eau *(f)*	*water*	le thé	*tea*

Higher only:

l'infusion *(f)*	*fruit tea*	le lait entier	*full-fat milk*
le lait demi-écrémé	*semi-skimmed milk*	la pression	*draught beer*
le lait écrémé	*skimmed milk*	la soucoupe	*saucer*

Things to Eat

l'agneau *(m)*	*lamb*	le biscuit	*biscuit*
l'alimentation *(f)* *Also* la nourriture	*food*	le bœuf	*beef*
l'appétit *(m)*	*appetite*	les bonbons *(m)*	*sweets*
la baguette	*French stick, baguette*	la boulette	*meatball*
		la brochette	*kebab*
le beurre	*butter*	le canard	*duck*

les céréales *(f)*	cereal
les chips *(m)*	crisps
le chocolat	chocolate
la confiture	jam
la crème	cream
la crêpe	pancake
le croissant	croissant
le déjeuner	lunch
délicieux	delicious
la dinde	turkey
le dîner	dinner, evening meal
emporter	to take away
les escargots *(m)*	snails
la faim	hunger
les frites *(f)*	chips
le fromage	cheese
les fruits de mer *(m)*	seafood
le gâteau	cake
la graisse	fat, grease
le hamburger	hamburger
l'huile *(f)*	oil
le jambon	ham
la liste	list
manger	to eat
la margarine	margarine
mélangé	mixed
mélanger	to mix
le miel	honey
les moules *(f)*	mussels
la moutarde	mustard
nourrir	to feed

l'odeur *(f)*	smell
l'œuf *(m)*	egg
l'omelette *(f)*	omelette
le pain	bread
le pâté	pâté
les pâtes *(f)*	pasta
les pâtisseries *(f)*	pastries
le petit déjeuner	breakfast
le petit pain	bread roll
la pizza	pizza
le plat cuisiné	ready meal
la poêle	frying pan
le poisson	fish
le porc	pork
la portion	portion
le poulet	chicken
la recette	recipe
le repas du soir	evening meal
le riz	rice
rôti	roast
rôtir	to roast
le sandwich	sandwich
la sauce vinaigrette	salad dressing
la saucisse	sausage
le saucisson	sausage (like salami)
le saumon	salmon
savoureux	tasty
la soupe	soup
Also le potage	
les spaghettis *(m)*	spaghetti

le steak	*steak*		le thon	*tuna*
Also le bifteck			la truite	*trout*
le steak haché	*burger*		la vanille	*vanilla*
le sucre	*sugar*		la viande	*meat*
sucré	*sweet*		la viande hachée	*mince*
la tarte	*tart, pie*		le vinaigre	*vinegar*
la tartine	*(slice of) bread and butter*		le yaourt	*yoghurt*

Higher only:

à la vapeur	*steamed*		goûteux	*tasty*
amer	*bitter*		la noix	*nut*
la casserole	*saucepan*		les nouilles *(f)*	*noodles*
cru	*raw*		l'œuf à la coque *(m)*	*boiled egg*
les cuisses de grenouille *(f)*	*frogs' legs*		*Also* l'œuf dur *(m)*	
dégoûtant	*disgusting*		l'œuf au plat *(m)*	*fried egg*
fait maison	*home-made*		l'œuf brouillé *(m)*	*scrambled egg*
la farine	*flour*		l'oie *(f)*	*goose*
le foie	*liver*		le pâté de foie gras	*goose liver pâté*
le fromage de chèvre	*goat's cheese*		la pistache	*pistachio*
fumé	*smoked*		le souper	*supper*
			le veau	*veal*

Accommodation

l'accueil *(m)*	*welcome (desk)*	le gîte	*holiday cottage*
l'ascenseur *(m)*	*lift*	l'hôtel *(m)*	*hotel*
l'auberge de jeunesse *(f)*	*youth hostel*	le lavabo	*basin, washbasin*
		le logement	*accommodation*
le bain	*bath*	le loyer	*rent*
le balcon	*balcony*	la pension complète	*full board*
la chambre	*room*	la piscine couverte	*indoor swimming pool*
la chambre à deux lits	*twin room*		
la chambre de famille	*family room*	recommander	*to recommend*
la chambre double	*double room*	la réservation	*reservation, booking*
la chambre pour deux personnes	*double room*		
		réserver	*to reserve*
la chambre pour une personne	*single room*	le sac de couchage	*sleeping bag*
		la salle de bain	*bathroom*
confirmer	*to confirm*	le savon	*soap*
le confort	*comfort*	la sortie	*way out, exit*
de luxe	*luxury*	la sortie de secours	*emergency exit*
la demi-pension	*half-board*	le tarif	*rate*
le dortoir	*dormitory*	le tarif réduit	*reduced rate*
la douche	*shower*	la tente	*tent*
l'entrée *(f)*	*entrance*	la vue	*view*
l'étoile *(f)*	*star*	la vue sur la mer	*sea view*
faire du camping	*to go camping*		

Higher only:

accueillir	*to welcome*	dresser une tente	*to pitch a tent*
la chambre d'hôte	*bed and breakfast*	héberger	*to lodge*
		prière de	*please (request)*

Buildings

l'appartement *(m)*	*flat, apartment*	l'immeuble *(m)*	*building (usually high-rise)*
le bâtiment	*building*	la maison	*house*
la cathédrale	*cathedral*	la maison des jeunes	*youth club*
la cave	*cellar*	la maison individuelle	*detached house*
le chauffage central	*central heating*	la maison jumelée	*semi-detached house*
la clé *Also* la clef	*key*	la maison mitoyenne	*terraced house*
la climatisation *Also* la clim	*air conditioning*	la mosquée	*mosque*
le commissariat	*police station*	le mur	*wall*
le couloir	*corridor*	le musée	*museum*
dehors	*outside*	la pièce	*room*
descendre	*to go down*	la porte	*door*
l'église *(f)*	*church*	la porte d'entrée	*front door*
entrer	*to enter*	privé	*private*
l'escalier *(m)*	*staircase*	la réception	*reception*
l'étage *(m)*	*floor (of a building)*	le rez-de-chaussée	*ground floor*
la fenêtre	*window*	la salle	*room, hall*
fermé à clef	*locked*	le sous-sol	*basement*
le grenier	*attic*	spacieux	*spacious*
historique	*historic*	les toilettes *(f)*	*toilets*
l'hôtel de ville *(m)* *Also* la mairie	*town hall*	le vestiaire	*cloakroom*

Higher only:

la caisse d'épargne	*savings bank*	la gendarmerie	*police station*
donner sur	*to look out over*	la maison de retraite	*retirement house*
l'échelle *(f)*	*ladder*	le vestibule	*foyer*
l'étagère *(f)*	*shelf*		

City, Town and Village

l'ambiance *(f)*	atmosphere	interdit	forbidden
ancien	ancient, former	*Also* défendu	
l'arrêt d'autobus *(m)*	bus stop	le jardin public	park
la banlieue	suburb	multiculturel	multicultural
la bibliothèque	library	municipal	public, municipal
le bruit	noise	le niveau	level
le bureau	office	le palais	palace
calme	quiet	le panneau	sign
la campagne	country(side)	le parking	car park
le centre-ville	town centre	le passage piéton	pedestrian crossing
le code postal	postcode	perdu	lost
l'espace *(m)*	space	la place	square
la ferme	farm	le pont	bridge
la fermeture	closure	public	public
la fête	holiday, festival, party	le quartier	district
la foule	crowd	la route	road
la grande rue	main street	la station de métro	underground station
l'habitant *(m)*	inhabitant	le taxi	taxi
habiter	to live	le trottoir	pavement
l'industrie *(f)*	industry	se trouver	to be located
industriel	industrial	le village	village
		la ville	town

Higher only:

l'arrondissement *(m)*	borough, district	la fontaine	fountain
le cambriolage	burglary	paraître	to appear
le canal	canal	le passage à niveau	level crossing
le distributeur d'argent	cash point	remarquer	to remark, to notice
entouré	surrounded		
les environs *(m)*	surrounding area		

Section 3 — Local, National, International & Global Areas of Interest

Environment

la boîte en carton	*carton*	le pétrole	*oil (from the ground)*
bruyant	*noisy*	la piste cyclable	*cycle path*
le centre de recyclage	*recycling point*	la planète	*planet*
le charbon	*coal*	pollué	*polluted*
la circulation	*traffic*	polluer	*to pollute*
cultiver	*to grow (plants)*	la pollution	*pollution*
les déchets *(m)*	*rubbish*	la poubelle	*rubbish bin*
le désastre *Also* la catastrophe	*disaster*	le problème	*problem*
détruire	*to destroy*	propre	*clean*
disparaître	*to disappear*	la protection	*protection*
économiser	*to save*	protéger	*to protect*
l'embouteillage *(m)*	*traffic jam*	le réchauffement climatique *Also* le réchauffement de la terre	*global warming*
en danger	*in danger*		
l'endroit *(m)*	*place*		
l'énergie *(f)*	*energy*	recyclable	*recyclable*
l'environnement *(m)*	*environment*	recycler	*to recycle*
l'espace vert *(m)*	*green space*	réduire	*to reduce*
faire du recyclage	*to recycle*	les ressources naturelles *(f)*	*natural resources*
fournir	*to provide*		
gaspiller	*to waste*	le sac plastique	*plastic bag*
le gaz	*gas*	sale	*dirty*
international	*international*	sans plomb	*unleaded*
jeter	*to throw*	sauver	*to save*
manque de	*lack of*	les transports en commun *(m)*	*public transport*
mondial	*global*	utiliser	*to use*
l'ouragan *(m)*	*hurricane*	la zone piétonne	*pedestrian zone*

Higher only:

abîmer	*to damage, to spoil*	l'énergie solaire *(f)*	*solar power*
améliorer	*to improve*	l'espèce *(f)*	*species*
augmenter	*to increase*	faire du compost	*to make compost*
l'avertissement *(m)*	*warning*	fondre	*to melt*
bénéficier	*to benefit*	le gaz carbonique	*carbon dioxide, carbon monoxide*
climatique	*climate*	le gaz d'échappement	*exhaust fumes*
la consommation	*consumption*	l'incendie *(m)*	*fire (emergency)*
construire	*to build*	la lumière	*light*
contaminer	*to contaminate*	les ordures *(f)*	*waste*
la couche d'ozone	*ozone layer*	la paix	*peace*
le déboisement	*deforestation*	la perte	*loss, waste*
les dégâts *(m)*	*damage*	produire	*to produce*
l'eau douce *(f)*	*fresh water*	ramasser	*to collect, to gather*
l'eau salée *(f)*	*salt water*	renouvelable	*renewable*
l'effet de serre *(m)*	*greenhouse effect*	surpeuplé	*overpopulated*
l'emballage *(m)*	*packaging*	le tremblement de terre	*earthquake*
endommager	*to damage, to harm*	trier	*to sort*
l'énergie renouvelable *(f)*	*renewable energy*	le volcan	*volcano*

Furniture

l'armoire *(f)*	*wardrobe*	le miroir	*mirror*
la chaise	*chair*	le placard	*cupboard*
le fauteuil	*armchair*	le rideau	*curtain*
le lit	*bed*	la table	*table*
le meuble	*piece of furniture*	le téléphone	*telephone*

Higher only:

l'horloge *(f)* *Also* la pendule	*clock*	meublé	*furnished*
les lits superposés *(m)*	*bunk beds*	le tiroir	*drawer*

Health

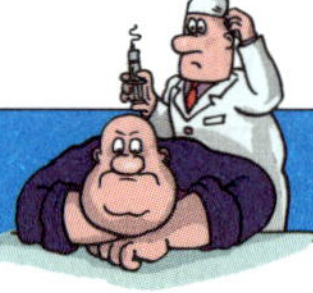

actif	*active*	avoir mal au ventre	*to have a tummy ache*
aider	*to help*	se blesser	*to get injured*
aller bien	*to be well*	casser	*to break*
aller mieux	*to be better*	la cigarette	*cigarette*
arrêter de *Also* cesser de	*to stop (doing something)*	le comprimé	*tablet*
s'arrêter	*to stop (moving)*	le coup de soleil	*sunburn, sun stroke*
l'aspirine *(f)*	*aspirin*	la crème solaire	*sun cream*
avoir mal à la gorge	*to have a sore throat*	dangereux	*dangerous*
avoir mal à la tête	*to have a headache*	se détendre *Also* se relaxer	*to relax*

la drogue	*drug(s)*	le médicament	*medicine*
se droguer	*to take drugs*	mourir	*to die*
en bonne santé	*in good health*	le non fumeur	*non-smoker*
en forme	*fit*	l'obésité *(f)*	*obesity*
équilibré	*balanced*	ordinaire	*ordinary, everyday*
faire de la musculation	*to do weight training*	paresseux	*lazy*
se faire mal	*to injure yourself*	la peur	*fear*
fatigant	*tiring*	la pilule	*pill*
fatigué	*tired*	prendre	*to take*
la fièvre	*temperature, fever*	le régime	*diet*
		rester	*to stay*
fort	*strong*	le rhume	*cold*
frais	*cool*	sain	*healthy*
fumer	*to smoke*	salé	*savoury, salty*
le fumeur	*smoker*	la santé	*health*
goûter	*to taste*	sentir	*to smell, to feel*
gras	*fatty*	se sentir	*to feel*
gratter	*to scratch*	le sommeil	*sleep*
la grippe	*flu*	tomber	*to fall*
grossir	*to put on weight*	tousser	*to cough*
le gymnase	*gym, gymnasium*	tuer	*to kill*
l'habitude *(f)*	*habit*	végétarien	*vegetarian*
l'hôpital *(m)*	*hospital*	vérifier	*to check*
s'inquiéter	*to worry*	vide	*empty*
maigrir	*to lose weight*	la vitamine	*vitamin*
malade	*ill*	vivre	*to live*
la maladie	*illness*	vomir	*to vomit, to be sick*
malsain	*unhealthy*		

Higher only:

accro	*addicted*	gâcher	*to spoil*
alcoolique	*alcoholic (person)*	hors d'haleine	*out of breath*
alcoolisé	*alcoholic (drink)*	ivre	*drunk*
l'alcoolisme *(m)*	*alcoholism*	la matière grasse	*fat (in food)*
avertir	*to warn*	mener	*to lead*
le cancer des poumons	*lung cancer*	la nourriture bio	*organic food*
crevé	*exhausted, tired*	la piqûre	*injection*
la crise cardiaque	*heart attack*	renoncer	*to give up*
déprimé	*depressed*	respirer	*to breathe*
désintoxiquer	*to detox*	le sida	*AIDS*
la douleur	*pain*	soigner	*to treat, to care for*
s'enivrer	*to get drunk*	le soin	*care*
épuiser	*to exhaust*	le tabagisme	*smoking*
s'entraîner	*to train, to practise*	le toxicomane	*drug addict*
essoufflé	*breathless*	*Also* la toxicomane	

Holidays and Festivals 

l'appareil photo *(m)*	*camera*		le Jour de l'An	*New Year's Day*
se baigner	*to go bathing, to go for a swim*		le jour férié	*public holiday*
le bloc sanitaire	*shower block*		la langue	*language*
le bord de la mer	*seaside*		le lundi de Pâques	*Easter Monday*
bronzer	*to sunbathe, to go brown*		la mer	*sea*
le camping	*campsite*		Noël	*Christmas*
le Carême	*Lent*		le Nouvel An	*New Year*
la carte postale	*postcard*		offrir	*to give (presents)*
la chambre d'hôte	*guest room*		Pâques	*Easter*
la colonie de vacances	*summer camp, holiday camp*		le parc d'attractions	*theme park*
la côte	*coast*		la plage	*beach*
l'emplacement *(m)*	*pitch (for a tent)*		le poisson d'avril	*April Fools' Day*
en plein air	*outside*		la promenade	*walk*
faire une promenade	*to go for a walk*		la randonnée	*hike*
la fête des mères	*Mother's day*		le sable	*sand*
la fête des Rois	*Epiphany*		la Saint-Sylvestre	*New Year's Eve*
la fête du travail	*May Day*		la Saint-Valentin	*Valentine's Day*
les feux d'artifice *(m)*	*fireworks*		le terrain de camping	*camping pitch*
les grandes vacances	*summer holidays*		les vacances *(f)*	*holiday(s)*
le jour de congé	*day off (holiday)*		les vacances d'hiver *(f)*	*winter holidays*
			la veille de Noël	*Christmas Eve*
			le vendredi saint	*Good Friday*

Higher only:

le défilé	*procession, parade*		le spectacle son et lumière	*sound and light show*
la messe	*mass*		les vacances de neige *(f)*	*winter holiday*
la Pentecôte	*Pentecost*			

In the Home

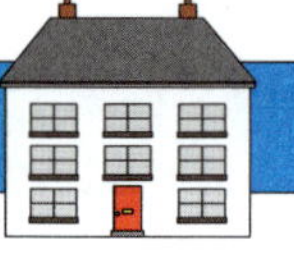

allumer	*to light, to turn on*	la lampe	*lamp*
l'aspirateur *(m)*	*hoover*	laver la voiture	*to wash the car*
commode	*convenient, handy*	le lave-vaisselle	*dishwasher*
confortable	*comfortable*	le linge de lit	*bed linen*
le congélateur	*freezer*	la machine à laver	*washing machine*
la cuisine	*kitchen*	mettre	*to put*
la cuisinière	*cooker*	montrer	*to show*
déménager	*to move house*	la nappe	*tablecloth*
le domicile	*home*	nettoyer	*to clean*
le drap	*sheet*	l'oreiller *(m)*	*pillow*
en désordre	*untidy*	l'outil *(m)*	*tool*
s'endormir	*to go to sleep*	le papier hygiénique	*toilet paper*
faire du baby-sitting	*to babysit*	passer l'aspirateur	*to do the hoovering*
faire du jardinage	*to do the gardening*	rangé	*tidy*
faire la vaisselle	*to do the washing up*	ranger	*to tidy*
faire le lit	*to make the bed*	renverser	*to knock over*
faire le ménage	*to do the housework*	réparer	*to repair*
le four	*oven*	repasser	*to iron*
le four à micro-ondes Also le micro-ondes	*microwave*	le robinet	*tap*
le frigo	*fridge*	la salle à manger	*dining room*
le garage	*garage*	la salle de séjour	*living room*
garder	*to keep, to look after*	le salon	*lounge*
		le sofa	*sofa*
		le tableau	*picture, board*
		le téléviseur	*television (set)*
l'image *(f)*	*picture*	tirer	*to pull*

Higher only:

le bricolage	*DIY*	éteindre	*to turn off (the lights)*
le cabinet de travail	*study*	le foyer	*home*
couvrir	*to cover*	la moquette	*carpet*

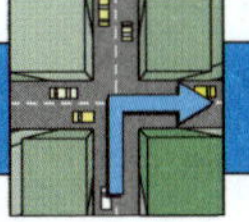

Location and Distance

à droite	*on the right*	là-bas	*over there*
à gauche	*on the left*	loin	*far (away)*
à l'extérieur	*outside*	le milieu	*middle*
à l'intérieur	*inside*	le nord	*north*
chez	*at (someone's house)*	nulle part	*nowhere*
continuez	*continue*	l'ouest *(m)*	*west*
de chaque côté	*on each side*	par	*through*
la direction	*direction*	partout	*everywhere*
en bas	*below, underneath*	proche	*close*
en haut	*above*	quelque part	*somewhere*
l'est *(m)*	*east*	situé	*situated*
ici	*here*	le sud	*south*
inférieur	*lower, inferior*	tournez à droite	*turn right*
intérieur	*inside, inner, internal*	tournez à gauche	*turn left*
le kilomètre	*kilometre*	tout droit	*straight on*
là	*there*	tout près	*really near*
		toutes directions	*all directions, all traffic*

Higher only:

là-haut	*up there*

Nature

agricole	*agricultural*	le lac	*lake*
l'arbre *(m)*	*tree*	la lune	*moon*
le champ	*field*	la montagne	*mountain*
le chemin	*path, way*	la nature	*nature*
la colline	*hill*	l'océan *(m)*	*ocean*
le feu	*fire*	le parc	*park*
la fleur	*flower*	la pelouse	*lawn, grass*
le fleuve	*river (that flows into the sea)*	pittoresque	*picturesque*
		la plante	*plant*
la forêt	*forest*	la rivière	*river (that flows into another river)*
l'île *(f)*	*island*		
l'inondation *(f)*	*flood*		
le jardin	*garden*	la terre	*earth, ground*
le jardin publique	*public gardens, park*		

Higher only:

l'espèce *(f)*	*species, sort, kind*	le paysage	*countryside*
l'herbe *(f)*	*grass*	le sommet	*summit*
inonder	*to flood*	la vague	*wave*
la marée	*tide*	le zoo	*zoo*
		Also le jardin zoologique	

Places

à l'étranger	*abroad*	le Danemark	*Denmark*
africain	*African*	danois	*Danish*
l'Afrique *(f)*	*Africa*	le département	*administrative district, county*
l'Algérie *(f)*	*Algeria*	Douvres	*Dover*
algérien	*Algerian*	le drapeau	*flag*
l'Allemagne *(f)*	*Germany*	écossais	*Scottish*
allemand	*German*	l'Écosse *(f)*	*Scotland*
les Alpes *(f)*	*Alps*	Édimbourg	*Edinburgh*
américain	*American*	l'Espagne *(f)*	*Spain*
l'Amérique *(f)*	*America*	espagnol	*Spanish*
l'Amérique du Nord *(f)*	*North America*	les États-Unis *(m)*	*United States*
l'Amérique du Sud *(f)*	*South America*	l'Europe *(f)*	*Europe*
anglais	*English*	européen	*European*
l'Angleterre *(f)*	*England*	la France	*France*
l'Asie *(f)*	*Asia*	gallois	*Welsh*
l'Atlantique *(m)*	*Atlantic Ocean*	la Grande-Bretagne	*Great Britain*
l'Australie *(f)*	*Australia*	grec	*Greek*
l'Autriche *(f)*	*Austria*	la Grèce	*Greece*
autrichien	*Austrian*	la Guyane	*French Guiana*
belge	*Belgian*	hollandais	*Dutch*
la Belgique	*Belgium*	la Hollande	*Holland*
la Bourgogne	*Burgundy*	l'Inde *(f)*	*India*
la Bretagne	*Brittany*	indien	*Indian*
britannique	*British*	irlandais	*Irish*
le Canada	*Canada*	l'Irlande *(f)*	*Ireland*
canadien	*Canadian*	l'Irlande du Nord *(f)*	*Northern Ireland*
la Chine	*China*	l'Italie *(f)*	*Italy*
chinois	*Chinese*	italien	*Italian*
la Corse	*Corsica*	le Japon	*Japan*
corse	*Corsican*		

japonais	*Japanese*	polonais	*Polish*
Londres	*London*	portugais	*Portuguese*
la Manche	*English Channel*	le Portugal	*Portugal*
le Maroc	*Morocco*	la province	*province*
marocain	*Moroccan*	les Pyrénées *(f)*	*Pyrenees*
le Massif Central	*Central France*	la région	*region*
la Méditerranée	*Mediterranean*	la Réunion	*Réunion*
le Midi	*south of France*	le Royaume-Uni	*United Kingdom*
le monde	*world*	russe	*Russian*
la Normandie	*Normandy*	la Russie	*Russia*
le Pakistan	*Pakistan*	le Sénégal	*Senegal*
pakistanais	*Pakistani*	la Suisse	*Switzerland*
le pays	*country*	suisse	*Swiss*
le Pays de Galles	*Wales*	la Tunisie	*Tunisia*
le Pays-Bas	*Netherlands*	tunisien	*Tunisian*
la Picardie	*Picardy*	turc	*Turkish*
la Pologne	*Poland*	la Turquie	*Turkey*

Social Issues

l'ado *(m/f)* *Also* l'adolescent *(m)*	*teenager,* *young person*	combattre	*to combat*
âgé	*old, aged*	le commerce équitable	*fair trade*
l'association caritative *(f)* *Also* l'organisation charitable *(f)*	*charity*	se comporter	*to behave*
		le dommage	*pity, shame*
		l'égalité *(f)*	*equality*
attaquer	*to attack*	l'état *(m)*	*state*
avoir peur	*to be afraid*	la famine	*famine*

la grève	strike
la guerre	war
il faut	you have to, it is necessary to
important	important
impossible	impossible
inclus	included
injuste	unfair
l'instruction civique *(f)*	citizenship
la jeunesse	youth
obliger	to oblige, to force
l'organisation caritative *(f)*	charity
la pauvreté	poverty
les personnes défavorisées *(f)*	underprivileged people
le Premier Ministre	Prime Minister
prévenir	to avoid, to prevent, to warn
la priorité	priority
la réduction	reduction
la reine	queen
responsable	responsible
le roi	king
sans-abri	homeless
la sécheresse	drought
la sécurité	security
le sondage	opinion poll, survey
le taux	rate
tout le monde	everybody
typique	typical
l'urgence *(f)*	emergency
le vandalisme	vandalism
le vol	theft
voler	to steal
le voleur	thief

Higher only:

affamé	starving
agresser	to mug
l'attaque *(f)*	attack
au profit de	in aid of
la bande	gang
la bonne action	good deed
déchirer	to tear
désavantager	to disadvantage
la dette	debt
la discrimination	discrimination
les droits de l'homme *(m)*	human rights
effrayant	scary, frightening
égal	equal
l'enquête *(f)*	inquiry, inquest
envahir	to invade
l'espionnage *(m)*	spying
les exclus *(m)*	outcasts, socially excluded people
le harcèlement	harassment

harceler	*to harass*	réfléchir	*to think, to reflect*
illégal	*illegal*	le réfugié	*refugee*
l'immigré *(m)*	*immigrant*	la retraite	*retirement*
les incivilités *(f)*	*antisocial behaviour*	sexiste	*sexist*
inconnu	*unknown*	soutenir	*to support*
s'inquiéter	*to worry*	supprimer	*to eliminate*
la loi	*law*	survivre	*to survive*
lutter	*to struggle*	le témoin	*witness*
mal nourri	*malnourished*	tenter	*to attempt*
la manifestation	*demonstration, protest*	le travail volontaire	*voluntary work*
menacer	*to threaten*	le troisième âge	*old age*
le mineur	*underage person*	valoir mieux	*to be better*
les produits bio *(m)*	*organic products*	la vente de charité	*charity sale*
le racisme	*racism*	la victime	*victim*
raciste	*racist*	le volontaire	*volunteer*
réaliser	*to realise*	le voyou	*delinquent, yob*

Tourism

French	English
à l'étranger	*abroad*
l'aire de jeux *(f)*	*play area*
l'aventure *(f)*	*adventure*
la brochure	*brochure*
le bureau des renseignements	*information office*
le château	*castle*
chercher	*to look for*
commercial	*commercial*
s'échapper	*to escape*
l'étranger *(m)*	*foreigner, stranger*
l'euro *(m)*	*euro*
l'excursion *(f)*	*trip*
fermé	*closed*
la frontière	*border*
la galerie d'art	*art gallery*
la liste des prix	*price list*
le monument	*monument*
l'office de tourisme *(m)* Also le syndicat d'initiative	*tourist information office*
le plan de ville Also le plan de la ville	*map of the town*
les renseignements *(m)*	*information*
le séjour	*stay*
le site touristique Also l'attraction *(f)*	*tourist attraction*
le souvenir	*souvenir*
la station de ski	*ski resort*
le tour	*tour*
le tourisme	*tourism*
le touriste Also la touriste	*tourist*
touristique	*tourist (adjective)*
la visite	*visit, tour*
la visite guidée	*guided tour*
visiter	*to visit*

Higher only:

le contrôle de passeport	*passport control*
l'enregistrement *(m)*	*check-in*
la foire	*fair*
l'hospitalité *(f)*	*hospitality*
jumelé	*twinned*
la location de vélos	*bike hire*
séjourner	*to stay*
la station balnéaire	*seaside resort*
le taux de change	*exchange rate*
le voyage organisé	*package holiday*

Transport

à pied	*on foot*	la ligne	*line, route*
aller à pied	*to walk*	marcher	*to walk*
l'aller-retour *(m)*	*return*	le métro	*metro, underground*
l'aller-simple *(m)*	*single*	la mobylette	*moped*
l'arrivée *(f)*	*arrival*	monter	*to climb, to get on*
l'autobus *(m)*	*bus*	la moto	*motorbike*
l'autoroute *(f)*	*motorway*	le moyen de transport	*means of transport*
l'avion *(m)*	*plane*	le navire	*ship*
le bateau	*boat*	la panne	*breakdown*
le camion	*lorry*	le permis	*licence*
le car	*coach*	le permis de conduire	*driving licence*
le carrefour	*crossroads*	le piéton	*pedestrian*
la carte routière	*road map*	le poids lourd	*heavy-goods (vehicle)*
le chemin de fer	*railway*	le quai	*platform*
composter	*to validate (a ticket)*	rapide	*fast*
le conducteur	*driver*	le retour	*return (journey)*
conduire	*to drive*	le rond-point	*roundabout*
le délai	*time period*	rouler	*to go along (in a car)*
le départ	*departure*	la rue	*street*
l'essence *(f)*	*petrol*	sens interdit	*no entry*
l'essence sans plomb *(f)*	*unleaded petrol*	sens unique	*one way*
le ferry	*ferry*	stationner *Also* se garer	*to park*
les feux *(m)*	*traffic lights*	suivre	*to follow*
la gare	*station*	tourner	*to turn*
la gare routière	*coach station*	le train	*train*
le gasoil	*diesel*		
le guichet	*ticket office*		
l'horaire *(m)*	*timetable*		
lentement	*slowly*		

le tramway	*tram*	la vitesse	*speed, gear*
les transports en commun *(m)*	*public transport*	la voiture *Also* l'auto *(f)*	*car*
le véhicule	*vehicle*	vous allez à pied?	*are you going on foot?*

Higher only:

la ceinture de sécurité	*seatbelt*	l'hélicoptère *(m)*	*helicopter*
diriger	*to direct*	l'intersection *(f)*	*junction*
doubler	*to overtake*	la limitation de vitesse	*speed limit*
écraser	*to run over*	les phares *(m)*	*headlights*
l'express *(m)*	*fast train*	ralentir	*to slow down*
le frein	*brake*	stationnement interdit	*no parking*
freiner	*to brake*	le transport aérien	*air transport*

Travel

l'aéroport *(m)*	*airport*	le contrôle des passeports	*passport control*
l'agence de voyages *(f)*	*travel agency*	le contrôleur	*ticket inspector*
attacher	*to attach*	la correspondance	*connection*
les bagages *(m)*	*luggage*	défaire la valise	*to unpack a suitcase*
le buffet	*snack bar*		
la caravane	*caravan*	descendre de	*to get out of*
le carnet	*book of tickets*	la destination	*destination*
la classe	*class*	direct	*direct*
le compartiment	*compartment*	la douane	*customs*
la consigne	*left luggage*	l'étape *(f)*	*stage (of a journey)*

faire la valise	*to pack a suitcase*	revenir	*to come back*
la location	*rental, hire*	le sac à dos	*rucksack, backpack*
la location de voiture	*car rental, car hire*	la salle d'attente	*waiting room*
louer	*to rent, to hire*	la station service	*service station*
se mettre en route	*to take to the road, to get going*	se terminer	*to end*
		le trajet	*journey*
monter dans	*to get into*	la traversée	*crossing*
partir	*to leave, to go*	traverser	*to cross*
le passager	*passenger*	valable	*valid*
le péage	*toll, tollbooth*	la valise	*suitcase*
le port	*port*	le vol	*flight*
prêt	*ready*	le voyage *Also* le trajet	*journey*
quitter	*to leave (a place)*	voyager	*to travel*
rater	*to miss (e.g. train)*	le voyageur	*traveller*
		le wagon-lit	*sleeping car*

Higher only:

atterrir	*to land*	manquer	*to miss*
la croisière	*cruise*	la portière	*door*
décoller	*to take off*	traduire	*to translate*
embarquer	*to board*	le Tunnel sous la Manche	*Channel Tunnel*
en provenance de	*coming from*		
l'heure de pointe *(f)*	*rush hour*		

Weather

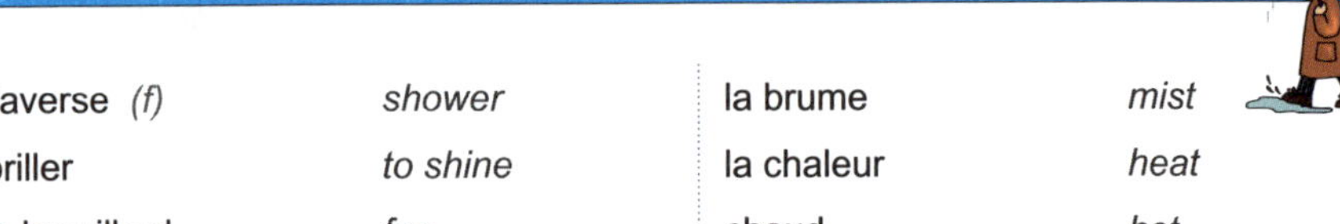

l'averse *(f)*	*shower*	la brume	*mist*
briller	*to shine*	la chaleur	*heat*
le brouillard	*fog*	chaud	*hot*

le ciel	*sky*	le nuage	*cloud*
le climat	*climate*	nuageux	*cloudy*
couvert	*overcast*	l'ombre *(f)*	*shadow, shade*
le degré	*degree*	l'orage *(m)*	*storm (thunder)*
doux	*mild, soft*	orageux	*stormy*
l'éclair *(m)*	*lightning*	pleuvoir	*to rain*
l'éclaircie *(f)*	*sunny interval*	la pluie	*rain*
ensoleillé	*sunny*	pluvieux	*rainy*
faire beau	*to be nice weather*	les prévisions météo *(f)*	*weather forecast*
		sec	*dry*
faire mauvais	*to be bad weather*	le soleil	*sun*
		la température	*temperature*
froid	*cold*	la température maximale	*highest temperature*
geler	*to freeze*		
la glace	*ice*	la température minimale	*lowest temperature*
humide	*wet, damp*		
il y a des éclairs	*there's lightning*	la tempête	*storm (wind)*
la météo	*weather forecast*	le temps	*time, weather*
mouillé	*wet*	le tonnerre	*thunder*
la neige	*snow*	tremper	*to soak*
neiger	*to snow*	le vent	*wind*

Higher only:

brumeux	*misty*	la température élevée	*high temperature*
s'éclaircir	*to brighten up*	la température moyenne	*average temperature*
la grêle	*hail*		
grêler	*to hail*	tiède	*tepid, lukewarm*
incertain	*uncertain*	variable	*changeable*
la température basse	*low temperature*		

Future Plans

l'ambition *(f)*	ambition		expérimenté	experienced
l'année sabbatique *(f)*	gap year		faire des études	to study
l'avenir *(m)*	future		mériter	to deserve
avoir l'intention de	to intend to		mettre de l'argent de côté	to save money
bien payé	well paid		l'occasion *(f)*	opportunity
le cauchemar	nightmare		prévu	foreseen, planned
certainement	certainly			
le certificat	certificate		le projet	plan, project
le conseiller d'orientation	careers adviser		les projets pour l'avenir *(m)*	future plans
craindre	to fear		le rêve	dream
décider	to decide		rêver	to dream
devenir	to become		souhaiter	to wish
le diplôme	qualification		l'université *(f)*	university
l'entrevue *(f)*	interview			

Higher only:

assurer	to assure, to insure		l'établissement *(m)*	establishment
la confiance	confidence		les études universitaires *(f)*	higher education
conseiller	to advise		la faculté	faculty, university
le débouché	prospect		former	to train
élargir	to widen		la licence	degree (university)
empêcher	to prevent			
l'enseignement *(m)*	teaching		la médecine	medicine
l'espoir *(m)*	hope		le souci	worry

Jobs

l'acteur *(m)*	*actor*
l'actrice *(f)*	*actress*
l'agent de police *(m)*	*police officer*
l'agriculteur *(m)*	*farmer*
l'architecte *(m)* Also l'architecte *(f)*	*architect*
l'artiste *(m)*	*artist*
le boucher Also la bouchère	*butcher*
le boulanger Also la boulangère	*baker*
le caissier Also la caissière	*cashier, checkout assistant*
le chauffeur	*driver (e.g. of a taxi)*
le coiffeur Also la coiffeuse	*hairdresser*
le concierge Also la concierge	*caretaker*
le cuisinier Also la cuisinière	*cook*
le dentiste Also la dentiste	*dentist*
le dessinateur	*designer*
le docteur	*doctor (non-medical)*
l'électricien *(m)* Also l'électricienne *(f)*	*electrician*
l'emploi *(m)*	*job*
l'enseignant *(m)* Also l'enseignante *(f)*	*teacher*
l'épicier *(m)* Also l'épicière *(f)*	*grocer*
le facteur	*postman*
la factrice	*postwoman*
faire du baby-sitting	*to babysit*
le fermier Also la fermière	*farmer*
le fonctionnaire Also la fonctionnaire	*civil servant*
l'homme d'affaires *(m)*	*businessman*
l'hôtesse de l'air *(f)*	*air hostess*
l'infirmier *(m)* Also l'infirmière *(f)*	*nurse*
l'informaticien *(m)* Also l'informaticienne *(f)*	*computer scientist*
l'ingénieur *(m)*	*engineer*
le journaliste Also la journaliste	*journalist*
le maçon	*builder*
le maître Also la maîtresse	*teacher (primary school only)*
le mécanicien Also la mécanicienne	*mechanic*
le médecin	*doctor (medical)*
le musicien Also la musicienne	*musician*
le petit job	*part-time job*
le pharmacien Also la pharmacienne	*pharmacist*
le plombier	*plumber*
le poète	*poet*
le policier Also le gendarme	*policeman*
la policière Also la gendarme	*policewoman*

le pompier	*fireman*
le programmeur	*programmer*
le réceptionniste	*receptionist*
le représentant *Also* la représentante	*rep(resentative)*
le secrétaire *Also* la secrétaire	*secretary*
le serveur *Also* la serveuse	*waiter, waitress*

le steward	*air steward*
le technicien *Also* la technicienne	*technician*
le vendeur *Also* la vendeuse	*salesman, saleswoman*
le vétérinaire *Also* la vétérinaire	*vet*

Higher only:

l'auteur *(m)*	*author*
l'avocat *(m)* *Also* l'avocate *(f)*	*lawyer, barrister*
le comptable *Also* la comptable	*accountant*
le dessinateur de mode	*fashion designer*
l'écrivain *(m)*	*writer*
le fleuriste *Also* la fleuriste	*florist*

l'interprète *(m)* *Also* l'interprète *(f)*	*interpreter*
le jardinier *Also* la jardinière	*gardener*
le mannequin	*model*
l'ouvrier *(m)* *Also* l'ouvrière *(f)*	*worker*
le prêtre *Also* le curé	*priest*

School Equipment

les affaires *(f)*	*things, items*	la gomme	*rubber*
le bloc-notes	*pad of paper*	le livre	*book*
le cahier	*exercise book*	le livre d'école	*school book*
la calculette	*calculator*	la page	*page*
Also la calculatrice		le projecteur	*projector*
le cartable	*schoolbag*	le pupitre	*desk*
les ciseaux *(m)*	*scissors*	la règle	*rule, ruler*
la colle	*glue*	le stylo	*pen*
le crayon	*pencil*	le stylo à encre	*fountain pen*
le feutre	*felt tip*	le taille-crayon	*sharpener*
la fiche de travail	*worksheet*	la trousse	*pencil case*

Higher only:

bien équipé	*well equipped*	mal équipé	*ill equipped*
la cartouche d'encre	*ink cartridge*	le stylo bille	*ballpoint pen*

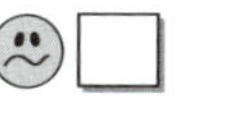  

School Life

l'année scolaire *(f)*	school year	encourager	to encourage
le bac	school leaving exams, A-levels	les études *(f)*	studies
		l'étudiant *(m)*	student
le baccalauréat	A-levels	étudier	to study
le brevet	GCSE	l'examen *(m)*	exam(ination)
calculer	to calculate	l'excursion scolaire *(f)*	school trip
le certificat de fin d'études	school leaving certificate	l'exemple *(m)*	example
		l'exercice *(m)*	exercise
la chorale	choir	l'expérience *(f)*	experiment
comprendre	to understand	se faire des amis	to make friends
copier	to copy	le groupe scolaire	school group
le cours *Also* la leçon	lesson	le groupe théâtral	drama group
		l'instituteur *(m)* *Also* l'institutrice *(f)*	primary teacher
demander	to ask	la journée scolaire	school day
le détail	detail	laisser tomber	to drop
la difficulté	difficulty	la liberté	freedom
le directeur *Also* la directrice	head teacher, director	le mi-trimestre	half-term
distribuer	to distribute, to give out	mixte	mixed
		la note	grade
le droit	right	oral	oral
l'échange *(m)*	exchange	parler	to speak
éducatif	educational	passer un examen	to sit an exam
l'éducation *(f)*	education	la pause *Also* la récréation	break
l'élève *(m/f)*	pupil		
l'emploi du temps *(m)*	timetable	perdre	to lose
en première	in year 12, in lower sixth	poser	to put
en seconde	in year 11	pouvoir	to be able to
en sixième	in year 7	pratiquer	to practise
en terminale	in year 13, in upper sixth	préparer	to prepare

le professeur	*teacher*	réussir	*to succeed*
le progrès	*progress*	réussir un examen	*to pass an exam*
rechercher	*to research*	réviser	*to revise*
redoubler	*to resit a year, to stay down a year*	savoir	*to know (a fact)*
le remplaçant	*supply teacher*	scolaire	*school (adjective)*
la rentrée	*return (to school)*	le semestre	*semester*
répéter	*to repeat*	le succès Also la réussite	*success*
répondre	*to answer, to reply*	travailler	*to work*
la réponse	*answer, reply*	travailleur	*hardworking*
le résultat	*result*	le trimestre	*term*

Higher only:

annulé	*cancelled*	passer en classe supérieure	*to move up a year*
l'assistant de langue *(m)*	*foreign language assistant*	pédagogique	*teaching, learning*
le car de ramassage	*school bus*	perfectionner	*to improve*
la connaissance	*knowledge*	poser une question	*to ask a question*
debout	*standing*	prononcer	*to pronounce*
se débrouiller	*to manage*	la prononciation	*pronunciation*
deviner	*to guess*	le proviseur	*headteacher*
doué	*talented, gifted*	la rédaction	*essay*
l'échec *(m)*	*failure*	la rencontre parents-professeurs	*parents' evening*
échouer	*to fail*	se servir de	*to use*
enseigner	*to teach*	surchargé	*overloaded*
épeler	*to spell*	le surveillant	*supervisor*
l'examen final *(m)*	*final exam*	la tâche	*task*
l'explication *(f)*	*explanation*	la traduction	*translation*
facultatif	*optional*		

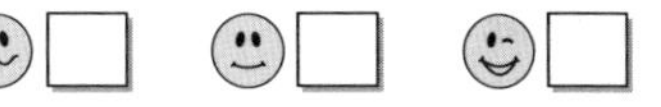

School Rules

absent	*absent*	écouter	*to listen*
apprendre	*to learn*	faire attention	*to be careful, to pay attention*
s'asseoir	*to sit*	permettre	*to allow*
assis	*sitting, seated*	présent	*present*
le bulletin scolaire	*school report*	le règlement	*rule*
défense de	*forbidden to*	travailler dur	*to work hard*
devoir	*to have to, must*	l'uniforme *(m)*	*uniform*
les devoirs *(m)*	*homework*		

Higher only:

l'autorisation *(f)*	*permission*	la retenue	*detention*
écrire des lignes	*to write lines*	sécher les cours	*to play truant*
être en retenue *Also* être collé	*to have detention*	se taire	*to be quiet, to stop talking*
l'injure *(f)*	*insult*		

School Subjects

l'art dramatique *(m)*	*drama*	le français	*French*
les arts ménagers *(m)*	*home economics*	la géographie	*geography*
la biologie	*biology*	l'histoire *(f)*	*history*
la chimie	*chemistry*	l'histoire-géo *(f)*	*history and geography*
le dessin	*art*	l'informatique *(f)*	*IT, ICT*
l'éducation physique *(f)*	*PE*	les langues étrangères *(f)*	*foreign languages*
les études des médias *(f)*	*media studies*	le latin	*Latin*

les maths *(f)*	maths		la physique	physics
Also les mathématiques *(f)*			les sciences *(f)*	science
la matière	subject		la sociologie	sociology
Also le sujet				

Higher only:

l'économie *(f)*	economics		les sciences naturelles *(f)*	biology
l'instruction religieuse *(f)*	religious education		les sciences physiques *(f)*	physics and chemistry
les langues vivantes *(f)*	modern languages		le thème	theme, topic
la matière obligatoire	compulsory subject			

School Types and Buildings

la cantine	canteen		le laboratoire	lab(oratory)
le collège	secondary school		le laboratoire de langues	language lab
Also l'école secondaire *(f)*			le lycée	sixth form college
la cour de récréation	playground		le lycée professionnel	technical college
l'école *(f)*	school		le lycée technique	technical college
l'école primaire *(f)*	primary school		la maternelle	nursery school
l'école privée *(f)*	private school		la salle de classe	classroom
l'école publique *(f)*	state school		la salle de sports	sports hall
le hall d'école	school hall		la salle des professeurs	staff room
l'internat *(m)*	boarding school		le terrain de sport	sports field

Higher only:

le centre de formation	training centre		la salle d'informatique	computer room
le pensionnat	boarding school			

World of Work

French	English
l'apprenti *(m)* *Also* l'apprentie *(f)*	apprentice
l'apprentissage *(m)*	apprenticeship
bénévolement	voluntarily
le boulot	work (familiar)
le candidat *Also* la candidate	candidate, applicant
la carrière	career
le chef	head, boss
le chômage	unemployment
classer	to file
le classeur	file
le collègue *Also* la collègue	colleague
le commerce	business, trade
les compétences *(f)*	skills
les conditions de travail *(f)*	terms of employment
la conférence	conference
la demande d'emploi	job application
le dossier	folder
l'employé *(m)* *Also* l'employée *(f)*	employee
l'employeur *(m)*	employer
enrichissant	enriching
l'entreprise *(f)*	business, company
l'enveloppe *(f)*	envelope
la facture	bill, invoice
faire un stage	to do work experience
la fiche *Also* le formulaire	form
la formation	training
le gérant *Also* la gérante	manager
gérer	to manage
l'heure du déjeuner *(f)*	lunch break
la lettre	letter
livrer	to deliver
mal payé	badly paid
le marketing	marketing
le métier	job
s'occuper de	to look after
par heure	per hour
le patron *Also* la patronne	boss
la pause-café	coffee break
la pause-déjeuner	lunch break
la pause-thé	tea break
poser sa candidature	to apply (for a job)
pressé	in a hurry
la pression	pressure
le produit	product
le propriétaire *Also* la propriétaire	owner
remplir un formulaire	to fill in a form
le salaire	salary
la société	society, company
le stage	course
le stage en entreprise	work experience

le timbre	*stamp*	l'usine *(f)*	*factory*
le travail	*work*	varié	*varied*
le travail bénévole	*charity work*		

Higher only:

s'adresser à	*to speak to*	la lettre de candidature	*cover letter*
l'atelier *(m)*	*workshop*	licencier	*to dismiss, to make redundant*
ci-inclus	*enclosed*	l'offre d'emploi *(f)*	*job advert*
le contrat	*contract*	la possibilité d'avancement	*opportunity for promotion*
l'entretien *(m)*	*interview*		
l'épreuve *(f)*	*test*	qualifié	*qualified*
le fichier	*file*	la réunion	*meeting*
l'impression *(f)*	*impression*	la signature	*signature*
s'inscrire	*to enrol*	suite à	*further to, following*
joindre	*to attach*		

Notes

Notes

Notes

FHV41